Jesus In My Practice

Jesus In My Practice

*Bringing the Questions of Jesus to
My Movement, My Meditation & My Mat*

Jody Thomae

JESUS IN MY PRACTICE: BRINGING THE QUESTIONS OF JESUS TO MY MOVEMENT, MY MEDITATION & MY MAT

ISBN: 9798763587821
Manufactured in the U.S.A.

Hebrew word definitions taken from Hebrew-Greek Key Word Study Bible: New International Version. Edited by Spiros Zodhiates. Chattanooga, TN: AMG, 1996.

Cover Artwork by Donna Godwin © 2018.
See donnagodwinartstudio210.wordpress.com

Dedicated to
Kim, Jillian & Amy
You've been with me through it all.

Contents

Before We Begin / 1

Questions Jesus asked...
Why were you searching for me? / 8
What do you want? / 12
Why do you involve me? / 16
Who by worrying can add a single hour to your life? / 20
What good will it be for a person to gain the whole world...? / 24
What do you think? / 28
What do you want me to do for you? / 32
Why are you bothering this woman? / 36
Which is lawful on the Sabbath...? / 40
Why are you so afraid? / 44
Who touched me? / 48
How many loaves do you have? / 52
Will you give me a drink? / 56
You of little faith, why did you doubt? / 60
Why do you look at the speck of sawdust...? / 64
Do you bring in a lamp to put it under a bowl or bed? / 68
Which of these three do you think was a neighbor...? / 72
If you love those who love you, what credit is that to you? / 76
Now which of them will love him more? / 80
Should not this daughter...be set free? / 84
Which of the two did what his father wanted? / 88
Woman, where are your accusers? / 92
What shall we say the kingdom of heaven is like? / 96
Where have you buried him? / 100
Are you here in this place hoping to be healed? / 104
Do you understand what I have done for you? / 108
Could you not keep watch with me for one hour? / 112
My God, my God, why have you forsaken me? / 116
Woman, why are you crying? / 120
Who do people say that the Son of Man is? / 124

As We Move Out From Our Mats / 129

About the Author / 135

Reference: YogaFaith Spotify Playlists / 137

Reference: Practice Journal Prompts / 139

Before We Begin...

If Jesus were my swami, my sifu or my sensei what might he teach me? Or better yet, what would I learn from him?

The person in the role of "Master Teacher" has many names in various practices of movement and meditation. In yoga this person is a Guru or Swami. In Tai Chi it is Taijiquan and in Qi Gong they might be called Master or Sifu. In classical dance, they might be called Ballet Master. In Japanese martial arts, Sensei is commonly used. In Buddhist meditation, one might be called Ajahn. And though they go by many names, they all serve the role as teacher and guide.

The person sitting under the teaching of this master might be called student, trainee, disciple, devotee or follower. They are there to learn not only the practice of movement or meditation, but also the philosophy of that practice as a way of life or "being" in this world.

In his own time, culture and setting, Jesus was known as a Rabbi, or *Rabboni* in the native tongue Aramaic. It meant "Teacher" and specifically a special kind of spiritual teacher who gathered followers called disciples. These disciples learned from him as they journeyed from village to village in the Ancient Near East. They learned not only from his teachings and the miracles he performed along the way, but also from the everyday journey we call life... the everyday tasks of eating, traveling, stopping to rest and to drink from a well. Mostly they learned from his interactions with others they met along the way.

But what does Jesus have to teach *us* as a Rabbi or Master Teacher in our *current* time, culture and setting? What can we learn from the questions Jesus asked as he and his friends journeyed the dry, arid lands surrounding Jerusalem? What does it look like to explore the teachings of Jesus to live a richer, fuller, more embodied life of grace, in harmony with others? A life that does not seek to cause harm to others? A life lived from a place of love rather than judgment?

More pointedly: How can we bring these questions of Jesus to our "mats" — our studios, our meditation rooms, our sacred spaces — in our own practices of movement and meditation? And how do those questions inform our lives? I believe that Jesus has much to teach us in this regard. This book and the reflections therein are just the tip of the iceberg in all he has to teach us as we make our way through both the big and little moments on this journey here on earth.

This book is for anyone interested in learning from the things Jesus said... whether you have grown up in a church or never set foot in one... whether you are devout in your Christian faith or other religious tradition that welcomes the teachings of Jesus or simply curious about the things he taught while he lived here on planet Earth... whether you consider yourself a seeker, a sinner or a saint, this is written with *us all* in mind.

This book is also for anyone wanting a more embodied spiritual path. One thing Jesus-followers believe is that he existed before the concept of earthly time within the Triune Godhead of Father, Son (Jesus) and Holy Spirit, and together they created the world around us. Somewhere around the time that divided human history into two halves (BC/Before Christ and AD/Anno

Domini), Jesus took on human flesh and entered the world as an infant child. This is known as *Incarnation,* and he was considered both fully human and fully divine in his earthly state.

Whether or not you believe in the Incarnation of Jesus, the theology of Incarnation is fascinating at the very least. The idea that the Creator of the Universe sent his Son to step down into the very world he fashioned means that the Godhead had a high regard for this world and the people they had created. Scriptures in fact tell us that it was for LOVE that Jesus stepped into the human race he had a hand in forming. You don't have to believe that Jesus was or is the Son of God to be curious about the idea that a Divine Creator would become human out of great love for the people he or she created.

The theology of Incarnation also reveals that the Creator had a high regard for the body in that a Divine God through the person of Jesus would take human form and live and walk on Earth. Throughout history, the Christian Church has not always treated the body with high regard. Christians were taught to subjugate "the flesh" through fasting, flagellation and other extreme measures (many other religious traditions follow these notions, as well). In an opposite vein, dancing, which had been part of the spiritual experience of the Hebrew people for thousands of years, was thrown out of the Church as evil. Over the years, movement and postures of prayer became suspect and ruled out of our Christian religious practice, with only a select few deemed permissible.

And yet... the human body was created to move, to dance, to sit in silence, to move in power and strength, and to form hand gestures and body postures of meditation, contemplation, prayer and worship.

So move we will... and learn... and connect mind, body, soul and spirit as we do.

Each writing is a reflection on a question Jesus asked as recorded in the Gospels (Matthew, Mark, Luke and John). Within each writing you will find:

- The question (as title heading).
- Passage: the Bible reference if you'd like to read the story in its context and entirety.
- Context: a brief explanation of the event surrounding the question, i.e., where Jesus was, who he was with, and what he was doing.
- Note: cultural notes of interest or relevance.
- Ruminate: thoughts, imagery or questions to ponder as you practice. Sometimes you will be asked to imagine yourself in the setting described and meditate on your own interaction or reactions as you imagine the story in your heart, mind, soul and body.
- Practice: suggestions for movements, gestures or postures that can be adapted for your own individual practice of movement or meditation, as well as a "breath prayer" (a cycle of inhales and exhales with specific intention) and a written meditation.
- Songs: song selections to augment the reading, the first listed is secular and the second sacred.
- Practice Journal: white space to process and record what was happening in your Body, Mind & Soul. Please see page 139 for practice journal prompts.

In the Reference section you will also find Spotify playlists that correspond to each practice. These are faith-based, Jesus-centered playlists of Christian worship music that I use when I teach YogaFaith classes. I can be found on Spotify as YogaFaith Jody and the full link is in the reference document. These are created for your use for your own private practice or as a teacher of faith-based movement.

It is my heartfelt desire that you will be blessed with both curiosity and peace as you ponder these words of Jesus. As we enter into our own individual and unique practices of movement and meditation, I will leave you with a traditional Blessing of Loving-Kindness...

May you be at peace.
May your heart remain open.
May you realize the beauty of your own true nature.
May you be healed.
May you be a source of healing for this world.

Shanti Shalom, Jody

Questions Jesus asked...

"Why were you searching for me? Didn't you know I had to be in my Father's house?"

Passage: Luke 2:41-52

Context: Every year the boy Jesus visited Jerusalem with the Hebrew people of his village for a religious feast called the Passover. When Jesus was twelve, as the family traveled home from the festival they realized he wasn't with the group. They hurried back to search for him only to find him in the temple courts "sitting among the teachers, listening to them and asking questions" (vs. 46). When his parents confront him, he asks,

"Why were you searching for me? Didn't you know I had to be in my Father's house?"

Jesus is seemingly nonplussed by his parents' obvious worry.

Note: These are the very first questions of Jesus *recorded in scripture.* However, we realize as a child, Jesus would have asked many questions before this. In fact, the passage says he's asking the teachers questions as he listens and learns.

Ruminate: There are some that say the soul is always searching until it finds its rest in its one true home, its one true Source. What is your soul's true home, its one true Source? For Jesus it was God, whom he called Father. And the fact that his parents were searching for him anywhere else than his "Father's house" was a search in vain futility. He would only be found in his true home.

These two questions of Jesus, the very first of many, cause me to pause and inquire of my soul three things: 1) What am I searching for? 2) Why am I searching? and 3) What do I expect to find? They might seem to be asking the same thing in three different ways, but these are three distinct questions for the soul. Take a moment to sit in silence with each of these:

What am I searching for?
Why am I searching?
What do I expect to find?

Practice: Spend some time exploring postures or stances that remind you of searching, perhaps with reaching arms or feet stepping forward. You might also want to explore one hand on the heart as the other reaches.

Take a deep breath...
    Exhale striving...
        Inhale hopeful expectation...

Our souls are searching,
always seeking,
always questioning.
Instead...
May we find our heart's true home
in something that cannot be built by man
in something that cannot be contained by walls.
    Peace... Hope
    Love... Mercy
        Divine Peace... Divine Hope
        Divine Love... Divine Mercy
And may our hearts remain open
    to Mystery,
        to Wonder,
        to Love.

Songs: *Home to You* by Sigrid
    Home to Me by Ben Smith

Practice Journal
Body ⇝ Mind ⇜ Soul

"What do you want?"

Passage: John 1:35-42

Context: As Jesus walks along the road, he passes by a prophet named John the Baptizer who refers to Jesus as the "Lamb of God." Two of John's followers begin to follow Jesus along the road when he turns around, looks them in the eye and asks,

"What do you want?"

They call him "Rabbi" (which means teacher) and want to know where he is staying so they can spend time learning from him. He replies, "Come and see," and these two men become the first two followers or "disciples" of Jesus.

Note: Jesus and John were cousins and had been born within months of one another. John the Baptizer had baptized many people including Jesus.

Ruminate: Imagine yourself at the scene with John and these men as Jesus passes by. Out of curiosity you tag along with these men who are following Jesus along the road. When he senses you following him, he turns around and asks you what you want? How would you answer? What are you looking to learn from Jesus? And I ask that question to everyone on the spectrum between "I basically know nothing about Jesus" to "I have learned about Jesus all my life." What do you want? What do you hope to learn? Are you willing to sit with him awhile, through the pages of this book, to see what he has to teach you?

In reply to your curiosity, Jesus replies, "Come and see." Won't you come and see? Doesn't matter where you are on this spectrum of learning about Jesus: you've heard things about him and come with those ideas, as well as other pre-conceived notions of who you think him to be.

But what if we could set those ideas aside for the duration of this book and purely came with curiosity and a willingness to listen? Whether you have no idea who he is or think you know everything about him, what if you simply set that aside and were willing to see and hear what he has to teach you, with fresh eyes and ears? What would that look like for you?

Practice: Taking a basic movement like a lunge or a squat, change it up and explore it with a "newness" and curiosity. Set aside all the pre-conceived notions of what a squat or lunge should look and feel like, and play with it a bit.

Take a deep breath...
Exhale the old...
Inhale the new...
I have looked at Jesus
through a specific set of lenses
without giving him a chance
to speak for himself...
Why?
What if... just what if... for a moment
I took off those lenses and looked again?
"What do you want?" he asks.
Good question...
let me ask it of myself,
"What *do* I want?"
I open myself to curiosity
to a willingness to learn
to wonder, childlike wonder...
"Come and see, child, come and see."

Songs: *Wonder* by Salt of the Sound
Wonder by Bethel Music

Practice Journal

Body ❧ *Mind* ❧ *Soul*

"Dear woman, why do you involve me?"

Passage: John 2:1-11

Context: Jesus and his family attend a wedding and the host runs out of wine. In this time and culture, this would've brought great embarrassment to the groom and bride. Jesus' mother Mary asks him to do something about it, and Jesus replies:

"Dear woman, why do you involve me?" NIV
"Woman, what does this have to do with me?" ESV
"My dear one, don't you understand that if I do this, it won't change anything for you, but it will change everything for me?" TPT

And then he explains, "My time has not yet come."

His mother apparently realizes Jesus can do something about this predicament. Having raised him, perhaps she knows he is capable of a miracle. But as the Passion Translation above indicates, Jesus knows a miracle as public as this will change everything for him. If he performs a miracle, news will travel fast. Despite his protest, he does decide to act, telling the servants to fill the containers with water. When they pour it out for the guests, the water has turned to fine wine.

Note: Jesus has only just begun to gather a few devotees, and has not yet started his "public" ministry to the people. Also note that "woman" is a term of endearment in that culture and context.

Ruminate: Think of a time when you were pushed into something before you were ready... or put on the spot to say something when you were unprepared... or were asked to get involved with something you never planned on...

How did you handle the pressure? How did you respond? This happens to each and every one of us at some point or another!

Consider how Jesus handled this situation of being put on the spot by his mother. He was candid with his mother, honestly expressing his hesitancy. Yet in the end stepped in with grace and mercy to save this family from great embarrassment. And as he stepped in, he began to tread the spaces of becoming all he was destined to be.

Practice: Think of a posture or movement that you don't think you're ready for. How can you explore adaptations or preparatory movements to help you begin to take on this challenge?

Take a deep breath...
Exhale the pressure...
Inhale new courage...
What if?
Just what if?
What if you simply try?
Destiny stands before you...
The world is ready!
"I am not ready,"
says the heart.
"I haven't prepared,"
declares the mind.
"This is new and difficult,"
asserts the body.
"Step into daring,"
whispers the soul.

Songs: *Becoming* by Jason Gray
Oceans / You Make Me Brave by Caleb and Kelsey

Practice Journal
Body ❧ *Mind* ❧ *Soul*

"Who of you by worrying
can add a single hour to your life?"

Passage: Matthew 6:25-34

Context: Jesus posed this question, along with several others, in the middle of a long section of teachings commonly referred to as the Sermon on the Mount. The crowds had gathered to hear his teachings, and they were impressed because he didn't teach like the other teachers, but as "one with authority" (7:29). In this section of the sermon, he is addressing worry and asks,

*"Who of you by worrying
can add a single hour to your life?"*

Jesus ends this teaching with this wisdom:

*"Therefore, do not worry about tomorrow,
for tomorrow will worry about itself.
Each day has enough trouble of its own."*

Note: This specific question is one of five he asked all related to worrying about the necessities of life, such as food and clothing. One of the other questions he asks is, *"Is not life more important than food, and the body more important than clothes?"*

Ruminate: What are the things that cause you worry? What occupies your anxious thoughts? We also spend a great deal of energy worrying about mistakes we've made in the past and what might happen in the future. It is very easy to fall into the trap of looking back with regret and being troubled over the days ahead. Yet when we stop and ask ourselves if this worry adds anything to our lives, I'm sure we can agree that this anxiousness adds nothing positive to our lives, let alone extends the days of our lives.

In fact, we know that stress and anxiety can actually shorten our lifespan.

Practice: Place one hand on your heart and the other on your belly. Notice the rise and fall caused by your inhalation and exhalation. When you truly focus on your breath, and only your breath, your mind, body and soul will stay squarely in the present moment. Let your breath remind you of the life you carry in you, *this very moment.*

Take a deep breath...
Exhale worry...
Inhale life...
As I breathe—
and with every breath—
I realize my regret must be released,
I pull myself from the pain of the past and
place myself in the present with Pure Peace,
I fracture the fear of the future,
I create a chasm between myself and chaos,
I distance my dilemmas with my dreams,
I will wisdom and wonder over worry,
I choose to cherish not cheapen every moment,
I agree grace and gratitude are greater.
Inhale
Exhale
Every breath a reminder...
I am alive!

Songs: *Inhale* and *Exhale* by Salt of the Sound
I'll Keep You Safe by Sleeping at Last
His Eye Is on the Sparrow by Casting Crowns

Practice Journal

Body ◆ *Mind* ◆ *Soul*

"What good will it be for a person to gain the whole world, yet forfeit their soul?"

Passage: Matthew 16:24-28

Context: Jesus is in a deep conversation with his disciples— the ones who have chosen to leave their lives behind to follow their master teacher. Although they are completely unaware of it, in this conversation Jesus is predicting his own coming death—a death in which he would forfeit his life on behalf of others. He teaches them that in order to save your life, you must lose it, and that whoever loses their life in service to Jesus, will find it. Then he asks these questions:

> *"What good will it be for a person to gain the whole world, yet forfeit their soul? Or what can anyone give in exchange for their own soul?"*

He is teaching them to live a life of sacrifice in service to others.

Note: The disciples have now traveled with Jesus awhile, so he is beginning to reveal to them the path of sacrifice that would lie ahead for Jesus. They are expecting him to overthrow the Roman rulers, but that is not his destiny. His disciples will not understand this life of surrender until he reappears to them after his death.

Ruminate: Reflect on a person (or perhaps a movie character) who gains wealth, power and prestige but loses their own soul in the process of gaining these things. What does it cost them? What things of true meaning and value do they lose as they grasp in greed for power and control? Now consider your own life... if you could gain the whole world—any prize, possession or position of power—but would have to give your own soul—your friends, your family, your integrity—in exchange, would it be worth it?

Now consider a person (or again, perhaps a movie character) who gives everything in sacrifice for a cause greater than themselves? What does it cost them? What worldly gains must they forfeit in order to walk a life of sacrifice and surrender? Again, considering your own life... what might you need to let go of in order to live a life in service to others?

Practice: Explore and compare grasping postures versus heart-opening postures.

Take a deep breath...
    Exhale worldly gains
      Inhale graciousness & generosity

What does it mean for me
to live in the trenches
side-by-side, should-to-shoulder
with others who forgo
prestige, possessions, position and power
in order to serve the least of these?
I open my eyes to
  see those in need.
I open my heart to
  graciousness
    generosity
      gratitude.
I open my hands to
  sacrifice
    surrender.

Songs: *Here I Am* by Shawn McDonald
   Surrender by Vineyard Music

Practice Journal
Body ᴂ Mind ᴄ Soul

"What do you think?"

Passage: Matthew 18:2,10-14

Context: The disciples come to Jesus asking which one of them will be the greatest in the Kingdom of Heaven. They've obviously been discussing the subject among themselves, and although they are jockeying for position, Jesus will have none of it. He calls a little child to come and stand among them. He begins to teach them not to look down on "these little ones" for they are great in God's eyes. Imploring them to consider others beyond themselves, he asks,

"What do you think?"

Which is followed by this question:

"If a man owns 100 sheep, and one of them wanders away, will he not leave the 99 on the hills and go to look for the one that wandered off?"

He tells them how the shepherd celebrates when he finds that single lost sheep. He equates the love the shepherd has for his sheep to the love God has for his own children.

Note: Jesus often used stories (called parables) to teach others about profound spiritual mysteries. Sometimes he explained the story and its application, and other times he let the story speak for itself.

Ruminate: Two things to consider. First, I love that Jesus is drawing his disciples out of their own selfish thoughts, and moreover, using a child to do so. He looks to the "lowly one"—a child without the knowledge to reason as an adult—and asks the supposed spiritually "mature" ones to think!

Second, this story asks us to think as well. The shepherd leaves behind his entire flock to find a single sheep that has wandered off. He searches until it is found and rejoices when he finds it. Have you ever felt like the one that has wandered off? Like everyone else has gone "the right way" and somehow you ended up on the "wrong" path? And now you wander—lost and aimless—expecting no one to ever come after you. Well... *what do you think?*

What do you think about a kind shepherd that leaves the rest to come look for you? Would you welcome his searching? And even more, would you welcome his rejoicing when he found you?

Practice: Explore poses or movements that take you from a posture of "hiding" to "being found"—like child's pose to camel pose in yoga, for example.

Take a deep breath...
> Exhale "loss-ness"...
>> Inhale "found-ness"...

When I wander away
away from my true self
> away from my destiny, purpose or calling
>> away from what it means for me to live
>>> authentically...
Will someone come find me?
Will loving-kindness make its way
> into the barren places
>> and pick me up
>>> and carry me home?
Come carry me home.

Songs: *Guiding Light* by Foy Vance & Ed Sheeran
Reckless Love by Caleb and Kelsey

Practice Journal
Body ∾ Mind ∾ Soul

"What do you want me to do for you?"

Passage: Mark 10:46-52 / Luke 18:35-43

Context: Jesus and his followers are on the road to Jericho. Hearing the noise of the approaching crowd, a beggar often referred to as "Blind Bartimaeus" asks what the commotion is about. When they tell him Jesus of Nazareth is approaching he begins to shout, "Son of David, have mercy on me!" Jesus' reputation obviously precedes him, and Bartimaeus wants a miracle! The crowd tries to shush him, and he refuses to let up and shouts even louder. Jesus stops and calls for him. Bartimaeus throws aside his beggar's cloak and jumps up to be brought to Jesus, who asks him,

"What do you want for me to do for you?"

Bartimaeus explains, "Rabbi, I want to see," to which Jesus replies, "Go, your faith has made you whole." And immediately the blind man's sight is restored.

Note: There are several innuendos in this story that point to awakening or resurrection. One of those is the Greek word *egerio,* which means to wake or raise from the dead, and in other scriptures, the word is used in that sense. Here it is translated as the command "On your feet" or "Stand up." In another allusion, Bartimaeus throws aside his beggar's cloak—which identified and labeled him in that society and "held" him bound to a life of begging—and jumps up. Like a man resurrected from the dead, he throws off his grave clothes and arises or awakens from his place of death.

Ruminate: Take a moment to think of places in your life where you feel held back—in need of awakening and resurrection. What are the roles or expectations that society has thrown at you; expectations that have perhaps held you in darkness and captivity; that have kept you from reaching your fullest potential? How have people "shushed" you or silenced you when you cried out for more?

Picture yourself there in the story with the crowds trying to quiet you as Jesus passes by. Imagine yourself shouting out, clamoring to be heard, seen, witnessed, attended to by one who has the power to help you out of your situation. Imagine he calls for you. What does it look like to throw off your "beggar's cloak" and jump up, approaching without sight to the voice that calls you forward? To arise from darkness into light? To resurrect from death to life? What will you throw off in this moment to awaken to the light that lives in you and the light that is meant to be shared with the world around you?

Practice: Work with two postures—one that represents darkness or a grave and one that represents light, awakening and resurrection. Move between the two postures, experiencing a move from darkness to light.

Take a deep breath...
Exhale darkness...
Inhale light...
I awaken to possibility
I throw off all that hinders
I arise from darkness
and step into light
I surface from the depths of death
and resurrect into life
I awaken to possibility

Songs: *Open Up Let the Light In* by Steffany Gretzinger
Let the Light In by Kari Jobe

Practice Journal

Body ➷ *Mind* ❧ *Soul*

"Why are you bothering this woman?"

Passage: Matthew 26:6-13 (or Mark 14:1-9)

Context: While traveling, Jesus and his disciples stopped at the home of a man named Simon. While Jesus was enjoying his meal, a woman came with an alabaster jar of perfume. She broke the seal and poured the contents upon Jesus' head, anointing him with the costly substance. The disciples became indignant, and began rebuking her saying, "Why this waste? The contents could have been sold and used for the poor." Jesus, aware of their disgruntled discussion, asks them quite pointedly,

"Why are you bothering this woman?"

and instead brands her actions a beautiful thing. He also foreshadows his coming death saying she was preparing him for his burial. And then he makes this powerful statement, "I tell you the truth, wherever the gospel is preached throughout the world, what she has done will also be told, in memory of her."

Note: Mark's gospel indicates that the perfume cost a full year's wages. This was not a small bottle of perfume bought on sale at the counter at discount store. This was a large alabaster jar filled with precious ointment. It was a great sacrifice and an extravagant act of worship.

Ruminate: Have you ever given a costly gift—one that required sacrifice? Perhaps not even a material gift, but a gift of the heart? What did that surrender cost you? Did people question your motives? Call you foolish? Consider it wasteful? Speak in judgment against you?

Now imagine Jesus was there with you in that moment saying, *"Why are you bothering this person? They have done a beautiful thing."*

How does it feel to have someone come to your defense? Picture him standing to defend your actions—actions that others consider foolish or wasteful. And not only that... he makes this bold statement that your actions would be remembered and your story of sacrifice would be shared throughout the world. What does it mean for you to give the offering of your heart to the world without fear of ridicule, judgment or condemnation?

Practice: Explore a posture or gesture of hands or heart extended in a sacrificial offering. Now retract or pull back away as if someone has insulted your gift. Then return again to the posture of hands or heart extended in offering with more confidence, emboldened by the knowledge that your sacrifice has long-lasting meaning.

Take a deep breath...
 Exhale regret...
    Inhale the beauty of your gift...
The blessing
 of an abandoned heart:
to give freely without fear
to give unreservedly without guilt
to give completely without restraint
and yet with wisdom...
  wisdom to know who deserves
   the precious offering of your heart
  wisdom to know the one
   who will come to your defense
    and tell the story of your sacrifice

Songs: *Atlas: Two* by Sleeping at Last
   Alabaster Heart by Kalley

Practice Journal

Body ❧ *Mind* ❧ *Soul*

"Which is lawful on the Sabbath: to do good or to do evil, to save life or to kill?"

Passage: Luke 6:6-11

Context: Jesus spent a lot of time in the synagogue on the Sabbath, the Jewish people's weekly day of rest—always under the watchful eye of the religious leaders. These religious leaders did not like what Jesus was teaching and were always plotting to catch him breaking one of the thousands of religious laws they had in order to shut him up. On this day there was a man there with a withered hand who had caught Jesus' eye. The leaders watched to see if he would heal him, which was considered "work" and not permitted on this day of rest. He knows their hearts and asks,

" Which is lawful on the Sabbath: to do good or to do evil, to save life or to kill?"

He then asks him to stretch out his hand, and when he does his hand is whole and complete.

Note: Because Jesus never touched the man, the religious leaders couldn't accuse him of breaking the Sabbath. While they were hoping to catch him breaking the law, he caught them instead on a technicality.

Ruminate: Take a moment to put yourself in the place of the man with the withered hand. Imagine you were in need and those who wanted to help could not because of a law, rule or policy. See Jesus finding a way, in spite of the restrictions, to help you, bringing wholeness where there was brokenness, deformity or loss.

Where have you tried to "do good" only to be caught in red-tape, rules and regulations? Allow your heart to be burdened by the frustration of not being able to "do good" for a moment. And now, turn your heart and mind towards an openness to creative ingenuity, clever imagination and resourceful innovation. How can we work together to be part of the solution that brings wholeness, restoration and goodness to those in need?

Practice: Experiment with a posture, position or pose that you often have difficulty transitioning into or out of. As you do, explore different approaches to entering and exiting that movement.

Take a deep breath...
    Exhale restriction...
       Inhale freedom...
The needs in this world are many,
  seemingly unsolvable on my own.
My hands feel tethered and tied,
    withered and tired.
And yet...
these hands can still hold and build and reach
my feet can stand and go and walk into places of need
my mind can think and solve and create new solutions
my heart can care and love and offer mercy...
May I be one who joins with others
  to fight for freedom
  to stand for justice
  to reach out with compassion and concern
And as I do,
  may my own withered hand be made whole

Songs: *Voiceless* by Matt Hammitt
 I Give Myself Away (Here I Am to Worship)
     by InSalvation

Practice Journal

Body ❧ Mind ❧ Soul

"Why are you so afraid?"

Passage: Mark 4:35-41

Context: It's the end of the day, and Jesus has spent the whole day teaching to crowds so large that he had to speak from a boat at the water's edge of a large lake in order to be seen and heard. As evening fell the disciples all loaded up in several boats, and they all began to cross to the other side. Suddenly, a violent storm rolled in—so violent they feared for their lives. Jesus however, slept peacefully on a cushion in the tossing waves. They woke him saying, "Teacher, don't you care if we drown?" to which Jesus responded by rebuking the wind and the waves. "Be still!' he said, and it became completely calm. He turned to his disciples and asked,

"Why are you so afraid?"

Note: The Greek word translated to Jesus' command to "be still" is *phimoo,* which means to muzzle or to reduce to silence.

Ruminate: Place yourself in the disciples' shoes (or boat, rather). How would you feel if your life was in peril, and you found the one person who could possibly do something about it asleep? I don't know about you, but I would be hurt and angry. I know I've asked Jesus a time or two myself, "Don't you care? Don't you see what's happening here? Won't you do something about it?" And every time, just like the disciples, Jesus seems to say back to me, "Why are you so afraid? I've got this. I've got *you!* I will protect you in the storm. Search for the silence. Find the stillness. It's there—always there."

What storms of life threaten to sink your own boat? What storms rage in your mind, your heart, your soul, your body? What if you dared to ask Jesus if he cared— cared enough to act on your behalf? What do you think might happen if you did?

Practice: Explore postures that leave your heart open, unprotected or vulnerable. Then experiment with postures that are more protective in nature. Alternate between the postures and notice how it feels in both your body and spirit.

Take a deep breath...
          Exhale the storm
               Inhale calm waters
My heart is...
    a boat on raging waters
    tossed and thrown
    from port to starboard
    from stern to stem
And yet...
    deep within...
My heart is...
    held in unexplained stillness
    there is only silent tranquility
    an inexplicable calm in the midst of storm
    not a ripple
        on the water
            of my soul

Songs: *Be Here Now* by Ray LaMontagne
       Nothing to Fear by The Porter's Gate

Practice Journal

Body 〜 *Mind* 〜 *Soul*

"Who touched me?"

Passage: Mark 5:21-43 / Luke 8:40-56

Context: The crowds are surrounding Jesus and pressing in as he and his disciples attempt to make their way through. A woman approaches who has suffered with some type of bleeding or hemorrhaging for 12 years. She has spent all that she had to find a cure, but now she believes that if she could just touch the hem of his garment, she would be healed. In the midst of the crowded bustling, she reaches out and in an instant is healed. But then... Jesus turns around and asks,

"Who touched me?"

The disciples think it's a ridiculous question given the crowds around him, but the passage says that Jesus knew that "power" had "gone out" from him. She reluctantly steps forward, falling at his feet in fear, confessing the whole truth and revealing his power had healed her. Jesus responds with mercy saying, "Daughter, your faith has healed you. Go in peace."

Note: In that culture and time, this woman would've been considered "unclean" due to her bleeding. As "unclean" she would have been ostracized by her community, unable to attend temple worship and living on the outskirts, an outcast, alone. By calling her "daughter" Jesus is reinstating her into the community that has rejected her.

Ruminate: This is a beautiful and remarkable story of healing and restoration. Twelve years she has suffered. Spent everything to find healing. Been rejected by her community. And then, in one touch of the hem of his garment, she is restored.

Imagine you are a part of this story. Perhaps you are the woman, a disciple trying to get Jesus to his next destination, someone in the pressing crowd, or even Jesus himself. How does the story unfold in your mind? The pressing crowd, the woman's desperation, the seeming ridiculousness of the question Jesus asks, the power leaving his body... what rises to the surface for you? What does this story say to you about restoration, hope, courage and faith?

Practice: Explore movements of pressing in and pressing through—through isometric exercises or through slow actions with engaged muscle groups, for example. Investigate pushing away with engaged muscles and then un-engaged muscles.

Take a deep breath...
               Exhale frustration...
                             Inhale restoration...
Press in
      through the crowds
      through the obstacles
      through the rejection that has stood in your way
      keeping you from receiving restoration
As you press, ask yourself,
      "What do I reach for?"
Are you reaching for hope?
      Courage?
          Strength?
             Healing?
And with what does your hand make contact?

Songs: *5 Hz Lokaha* by Wah!
      One Touch (Press) by Nicole C. Mullen

Practice Journal

Body ❧ *Mind* ❧ *Soul*

"How many loaves do you have?"

Passage: Matthew 15:29-39

Context: The crowds have gathered once again, this time near the Sea of Galilee, a remote location far from any cities. For three days solid the people bring their lame, blind, crippled, mute and other sick loved ones to Jesus to be healed. As the days pass, the scriptures indicate that Jesus' heart is moved to compassion, afraid to send them away hungry for fear they would collapse on the journey home. He turns to his disciples and asks,

"How many loaves do you have?"

The answer is seven, plus a few small fish. Even Jesus and his disciples are low on provisions. Yet Jesus sets to work. He starts with gratitude—giving thanks for what he has—and then begins to break the fish and loaves into pieces. In the end 4,000 are fed and there were still seven baskets of food left over.

Note: Crowd numbers in the Bible are always estimated and never include women and children. Often they were given as symbolic rather than for accuracy. Also note that the number of baskets leftover is the same amount as the original provisions. Note that in Christianity, seven is a holy number.

Ruminate: This question is rooted in a heart moved by gratitude and compassion. Although he has spent three days giving of his heart by healing them, Jesus sees the crowds, and still he longs to feed them, to fill their stomachs (and souls) with nourishment before he sends them on their way. What moves *your* heart to compassion? What needs do you see in the world that cause you to feel burdened? And better yet, what needs do you see that you might not have the means to do anything about? This question in particular begs us to start with what we have. What are the provisions we have on hand?

Think for a moment:
What *do* I have? What *can* I give?

And then... give thanks. Start with gratitude. Be thankful for what you have. Maybe you don't have money, but do you have time? Give thanks and then give it away. Maybe you can't give your home to the homeless, but do you have hands that can help build a home for another? Give thanks and then pick up a hammer. *Growth always begins with gratitude.*

Practice: Explore body or hand positions that communicate gratitude. Then, ones that communicate compassion and giving. Alternate between the postures or gestures you find.

Take a deep breath...
Exhale want
Inhale gratitude
I often live my life in scarcity and want
when in reality I have all I need.
In this moment, with every breath, I give thanks for all I have... not just material possessions, but the things that really matter... life... love... hands and a heart that can help in big and small ways.
As I offer gratitude...
I open my heart and soul to growth...
May I see new ways to offer compassion to others.

Songs: *Thankful* by Josh Groben
Overflow by Mary James

Practice Journal
Body ❧ Mind ❧ Soul

"Will you give me a drink?"

Passage: John 4:1-42

Context: Jesus and his disciples had been traveling several days and stop at a well outside a small town for refreshment. The disciples go to find food, and Jesus stays by the well. A woman comes with her water jug and lets it down for some water. Jesus asks her,

"Will you give me a drink?"

for he had nothing to lower into the well himself.

This question initiates a long conversation—one that included the Samaritan woman's questionable reputation. The woman tries to deflect with questions about worship and the coming Messiah. Jesus gently (and *without judgment*) confronts her and offers her a new source of water—*living water*—water that refreshes the deepest places of the soul.

As a result of this interaction, her heart is deeply touched, and she runs back to tell everyone of the man "who told her everything she had ever done." As a result of her story, many come to believe in Jesus as the Son of God.

Note: This question might seem like a very normal and benign one. However, it was extremely unusual and, in fact, controversial. First, in that time period, men never spoke to women in public. Second, the woman was a Samaritan, and in that day and age Jewish people did not associate with the people of Samaria. If Jesus had followed culture and custom, he would've never spoken a word to her, no matter how thirsty he might've been. It simply wasn't done.

Ruminate: What attitudes and beliefs keep us from interacting with others who are not like us... others who don't think or look or act like us? We might think we are above that, but we all hold prejudice of some kind in our hearts. Jesus purposely engaged someone whom his culture and custom dictated he shouldn't. As he did, it made room for a conversation that for this woman was life-changing... not because he preached at her, but because he was willing to open his heart to her and hear what she *wasn't* saying but certainly needed to share.

How can our hearts be more open to and accepting of others? When we offer our hearts in deep conversation with someone with whom we disagree... to really listen... and hear what they may or may not be saying... without judgment... *that is a true gift!*

Practice: What movement, posture or gesture represents "pushing away" to you? What represents "welcoming' to you? Explore pushing away prejudice and welcoming those in need of love, grace and acceptance.

Take a deep breath...
                Exhale prejudice
                          Inhale acceptance
"Will you give me a drink?" he asks.
        In truth... aren't we *all* thirsty?
Thirsty to be seen and heard...
                            understood and known.
May we be the first to break down the barriers that separate us from others. May we be the first to listen, to really hear the heart of another. May we open our hearts with love, as a BEaUtiful gift to the world.

Songs: *This Gift* by Glen Hansard
          Living Water by Gateway Worship

Practice Journal

Body ❧ *Mind* ❧ *Soul*

"You of little faith, why did you doubt?"

Passage: Matthew 14:22-33

Context: Here we find another story where the disciples are sent ahead on a boat and Jesus comes walking out to them on the water. In this story, Jesus has stayed back to attend to the crowds and then go to a quiet place to pray. Meanwhile, on the water, the disciples in the boat struggle to row against the buffeting waves. Jesus comes walking across the water to help them, encouraging them (literally, "Take courage"). When his disciple Peter asks if it's really him, Jesus tells him to get out of the boat and walk across the water. Peter does so and finds himself miraculously walking on the water.

But then... his near fatal mistake... he takes his eyes off Jesus. Fear fills him, and he begins to sink. As Peter cries out, Jesus catches him and says,
"You of little faith, why did you doubt?"
As Jesus climbs into the boat with Peter, the wind and waves settle, and his disciples are amazed!

Note: This is the second of two different walking on water stories found in the Bible. In the first, a violent storm arose, and we heard the question, "Why are you so afraid?" In this one, the wind is against them, and they are striving to row against the waves.

Ruminate: Jesus asks Peter to get out of the boat. This imagery has been used as a metaphor many times for those instances when we need to step out in courage. So we ask ourselves: "What 'boat' would I step out of? What seems impossible? What fears must I face to have the courage to do so?"

We might also want to consider the people we have surrounding us, supporting us. Who is calling us out of our boats of safety, out of our comfort zones? Who do we look to for encouragement—to speak courage into our hearts when we look at the wind and waves that threaten to undo our best intentions?

Practice: Press into movements of stepping out or stepping into. Then counter poses of stepping back or away. Now play with "two-steps-forward-one-step-back" as you consider living out the dreams you have for your life.

Take a deep breath...
   Exhale fear...
      Inhale courage...
   Exhale old ways...
      Inhale new dreams...
What miracle
  would I move into
    if I only had the courage?
What adventure
  would I advance
    if I gathered my strength?
What dream and destiny
  would I dance into
    if I dared to step out
      onto the waves
        and into the wind?
And what BEaUty
  would the world behold?

Songs: *Atlas: Six* by Sleeping at Last
  Sinking Deep by Hillsong Young & Free

Practice Journal

Body ∂ Mind ∽ Soul

"Why do you look at the speck of sawdust in your brother's eye and pay no attention to the plank in your own?"

Passage: Matthew 7:1-6

Context: Jesus is teaching a large crowd on a hill overlooking the Sea of Galilee in Northern Israel. He is addressing how we judge others. He teaches that we will be judged in the same way we judge others, and asks:

"Why do you look at the speck of sawdust in your brother's eye and pay no attention to the plank in your own eye? How can you say to your brother, 'Let me take the speck out of your eye,' when all the time there is a plank in your own eye?"

Jesus is obviously using hyperbole here, exaggerating to make his point. He goes on to say that we must address the "plank"—our own issues, imperfections and shortcomings—in our own eyes before we address the faults of another. He realizes that only by attending to our own "blind spots" can we "see" to help another.

Note: This teaching is found in a section of Matthew (chapters 5–7) commonly referred to as the Sermon on the Mount. The phrase "look at" above is from the Greek *blepo*, which means to look, be on the lookout, to direct one's sight towards an object, or to observe in citation of someone. "Pay (no) attention" is *katanoeo*, which means to consider, discern or contemplate.

Ruminate: How easy it is to see the faults of others and difficult to discern our own. We live in a shame-based culture (here in America, at least), where shame is used to manipulate and coerce people into behaving and thinking in certain ways deemed acceptable. Even those that perceive themselves to be spiritually, intellectually or socially enlightened can look down on others and judge them as ignorant or boorish, rather than simply unaware. More and more, we hear that instead of asking with disgust and condemnation, "What's *wrong* with you?!" we need to ask with understanding and compassion, "What *happened* to you?"

When have you recently thought or even said, "What's wrong with them?" And what if you considered instead, "What might have happened to them that they act or think this way?" Take a moment to consider, discern or contemplate the plank that might be hindering your own eyesight. Consider how you can look on others around you with more compassion.

Practice: Explore postures or movements that feel closed or judgmental and then those that feel open and accepting. Where do you hold judgment in your body? Where do you hold acceptance in your body?

Take a deep breath...
   Exhale prejudice...
     Inhale regard...
I remove the plank
I examine it and ask,
  "How did it get there?"
I consider my own story and offer self-compassion.
Then I look to the speck in another
I see it's not as big as I once thought.
I find compassion and mercy within
I see with new eyes.

Songs: *Lovely* by Sara Haze
  One & All by One Hope Project

Practice Journal
Body ❧ *Mind* ☙ *Soul*

"Do you bring in a lamp
to put it under a bowl or bed?"

Passage: Mark 4:21-25

Context: This is another of Jesus' parables: stories he used to teach, to illustrate a point, or to give the mind a truth to ponder. This one in particular is nestled between several other parables about seeds—in many ways it doesn't seem to fit. Jesus is talking about planting seeds in fertile and unfertile soil; unseen growth occurring underground; and the blessings of future harvests. And then he asks this question:

"Do you bring in a lamp
to put it under a bowl or bed?"

Of course, the obvious answer is no, a bowl would extinguish it, and placing a light with a flame under a bed would possibly burn the whole house down. In that culture it was placed on a lamp stand—a special place in the home where the light would illuminate the darkness.

Note: I wonder if this story is placed within these other stories of seeds to illuminate the truth found in the stories encompassing it?

Ruminate: Think of the seed germinating underground, awaiting its moment of growth in the dark, rich soil. As roots appear and reach downward to moisture and nutrients, a sprout merges and grows heavenward to sunlight. It breaks through the surface to find its source of light.

What truth is being illuminated in this current season of your life? Is there a light shining, shedding truth in the darkness? In the places where seeds are being planted? Places where there seems to be no growth or movement? Places where there is a harvest coming from months of waiting and hoping?

Practice: What gesture, form or posture can you take that might represent a seed underground? Is there a counter movement that might represent growth? Explore moving between these two gestures or movements.

Take a deep breath...
        Exhale darkness...
                Inhale light...
        Exhale stagnation...
                Inhale growth...

It appears as if there is only barrenness
    no movement
    no growth
But just you wait
    in the darkness
    the seed
        gathers its strength
    and when ready
    springs forth
    ready to reach for the light
    and turn its face
    to the blinding sun
It's coming...
    I promise...
        your moment in the sun

Songs: *I Am Light (528hz)* by Power Thoughts
                Meditation Club
Shine by Kimberly and Albert Rivera

Practice Journal
Body ❧ Mind ❧ Soul

"Which of these three do you think was a neighbor to the man who fell into the hands of robbers?"

Passage: Luke 10:25-37

Context: Commonly referred to as the story of the Good Samaritan, this is yet another parable of Jesus. Jesus told this story in response to a teacher of the Jewish Law trying to test him by asking how one would "enter the kingdom of heaven." Jesus turns the question back at him, but the man persists and asks Jesus, "Who is my neighbor?" Jesus then poses a scenario which is less metaphorical and more hypothetical in nature than his other parables.

He tells the story of a man beaten, robbed and left for dead by the side of the road. First, a Jewish priest and then a worship leader both pass him by before a Samaritan stops to tend the beaten man's wounds and arrange for his care. At the end of his story he asks the teacher of the Law: *"Which one of these three do you think was a neighbor to the man who fell into the hands of the robber?"*

Note: In the racist and classist culture of the Ancient Near East, Samaritans were considered one of the lowest classes of citizens by the Jewish people. The fact that the lowest class of citizens, rather than one of the religious leaders, stops to help the Jewish man left for dead is the rub of the story. It would have spoken volumes.

Ruminate: How can we be neighbors to others in this world? It's easy to be a neighbor to our friends and those we like, but in Jesus' eyes, that's not the true sign of a neighbor... that's not the true essence of kindness, compassion and mercy. The neighbor is one who stops to help... no matter who it is that needs help. It's easy to look the other way... to think that someone else will take care of those in need or that it is the government's or a professional's job to look after others... especially when the "others" aren't like us.

But Jesus defines a different way... a way where everyone, regardless of race or class, gets the assistance and compassion they need. Jesus would ask each of us to provide, protect and watch out for others that look, act, think and believe differently than we do.

Practice: Explore postures, movements or gestures that first indicate a "closed off" stance and then an open and giving stance. How does it feel to close yourself off versus open yourself up to the needs of others?

Take a deep breath...
            Exhale limited thinking...
                        Inhale open awareness...
I open my eyes to See
        those whom I have turned a blind eye to
I open my ears to Hear
        those who have cried out for help
I open my mouth to Speak up for
        those who have cried out for justice
I open my hands to Give generously to
        those who have less than I
Help me See, Hear, Speak and Give...
        Help me to See with Love, Hear with Love,
        Speak with Love and Give to others in Love.

Songs: *Us* by James Bay
        A Generous Heart by Tony Alonso,
                Chris de Silva & Liam Lawton

Practice Journal

Body ✺ *Mind* ✺ *Soul*

"If you love those who love you, what credit is that to you?"

Passage: Luke 6:27-36

Context: In this teaching, Jesus is sharing what it means to love not just your neighbor, but to love your enemy. He instructs us to "turn the other cheek" and to "do unto others as you would have them do unto you" (aka The Golden Rule). And of course, he wants us to go beyond simply loving those who are nice to us. He's asking that we bless those that curse us; give to those who take from us; and to repay evil with kindness. Then he asks,

"If you love those who love you, what credit is that to you?" NIV

"Are you really showing true love by loving only those who love you?" TPT

"Listen, what's the big deal if you love people who already love you?" VOICE

And I love the next statement in the Voice translation: "Even scoundrels do that much!" Jesus is really taking us to task on this one! But he certainly has a point: we spread love in this world only by being love. And if *we* aren't love, then who will be?

Note: The Golden Rule has its equivalent in most other religions. For example, in Buddhism they say, "Hurt not others with that which pains yourself." In Hinduism: "This is the sum of duty: do naught to others which if done to thee, would cause thee pain." And in Islam: "No one of you is a believer until he loves for his brother what he loves for himself."

Ruminate: Let's ruminate on this question of Jesus as quoted from The Passion Translation above:

"Are you really showing true love by loving only those who love you?"

In this world of vitriol and hate, I often see tee-shirts and social media posts about being love to those around us. But what does it mean to *truly* love, especially when we struggle or even flat-out refuse to be kind to those who act or think differently than we do?

What is brotherly or sisterly love anyways? And how does it play itself out in our day-to-day lives? And what credit is it to us if we only love those who love us?

Practice: Find and explore postures and movements that push forward (extension) and retract back (flexion) the solar-plexus area of the torso. In many mind-body traditions, the solar plexus region is known as the "power center." What does it feel like to explore this place in the body?

Take a deep breath...

Exhale hate...

Inhale love...

I ask myself
not
How am I loving?
but
How am I love?

Songs: *Light of Love* by Jai-Jagdeesh
A Prayer for Grace by Morgan Harper Nichols

Practice Journal

Body   ❧   Mind   ❧   Soul

"Now which of them will love him more?"

Passage: Luke 7:36-50

Context: We have already examined an account of Jesus being anointed in the question, "Why are you bothering this woman?" This story, told by Luke, offers another angle to the story. As the woman—described in this story as a "sinful" woman—anoints him, the complaining starts. Jesus begins to tell the story of two men that owed a moneylender—one owed $500, the other $50. The man cancelled both their debts because neither had the money to pay him back, and Jesus asks,

"Now which of them will love him more?"

to which the chief complainer answers, "I suppose the one who had a bigger debt." Jesus agrees and goes on to say, "The one who has been forgiven much loves much; and the one who has been forgiven little loves little." And then he sends the woman on her way with a blessing of forgiveness and peace.

Note: There are many who discredit the Bible due to discrepancies between stories without considering that each person there would interpret the events through their own lens, point of view and even vantage point in the room. Witnesses routinely give different accounts of the same incident.

Ruminate: Consider a time when you were accepted despite your past, your faults and your failings. Or perhaps a time when you "goofed up" and were offered "a pass"—mercy, compassion and forgiveness when you clearly didn't deserve it. How did it feel to be accepted as you are, without having to pretend you had it all together?

Now consider a time when you had an opportunity to accept someone despite his past behavior or her faults and shortcomings but refused to do so. What stood in your way? How could you have handled the situation differently—extending kindness where perhaps it was not deserved? That is certainly a very difficult task, isn't it?

How can we make a practice of extending loving-kindness and accepting people as they are, faults and all? This practice is one that takes great discernment and deep courage. A challenge indeed!

Practice: Consider movements and postures that challenge you or cause difficulty for you. How can you step into the challenge with discernment and courage, while still being cautious to care for your own self?

Take a deep breath...
　　　　Exhale intolerance...
　　　　　　　　Inhale loving-kindness...
I come as I am
offering loving-kindness to the places within
that may not deserve or warrant it
　　　but I come as I am.
I also look to others...
Help me accept them as they are
offering loving-kindness to the places
where they do not seem to deserve or warrant it
　　　but I see them as they are.
I am challenged
　　　But I am growing in grace...
　　　　　I come as I am.

Songs: *Fly* by Sara Groves
　　　　Much by Ten Shekel Shirt

Practice Journal

Body   Mind   Soul

"Should not this daughter of Abraham... be set free?"

Passage: Luke 13:10-17

Context: Jesus is teaching in the synagogue on the Sabbath. He sees a woman who is bent over, unable to straighten, and calls her to him. The scripture indicates she has been doubled over for 18 years, but Jesus speaks and declares, "Woman, you are set free," and she immediately stood up straight.

Now, of course, it's the Sabbath and according to the religious leaders, healing someone was considered "work"—and you are not allowed to work on the Sabbath. As we know, Jesus disregards these man-made sanctions, so the religious leaders are angry with him once more. Knowing their discontent, he asks not just one, but two questions:

> *"Doesn't each of you on the Sabbath untie his ox or donkey and lead it to water? Then should not this daughter of Abraham, whom satan has kept bound for 18 long years, be set free on the Sabbath day from that which bound her?"*

Note: The Greek for 'set free' above is *apolyo,* which means to set loose as from bondage or imprisonment. Further, the imagery in this passage paints the picture of this woman as a beast of burden—bent over, tied up, captive, bound by and bearing the weight of an enormous load.

Ruminate: Place yourself in ancient Israel, and picture this moment in your mind. Imagine this... Jesus does three things: he *sees* her; he *summons* her, and he *speaks* to her. This moment is all about her. And with one touch from

Jesus' hand, she *immediately* straightens—set free from that which has held her bound. With her "deformity," she would've been seen and treated as an outsider in ancient culture—for almost two decades! But in an instant her life is set right again. Jesus calls her "daughter of Abraham"—an expression of honor and a "reinstatement" back into her community.

Imagine being there, watching this miracle of inclusion, restitution and freedom take place. What emotions rise up within as you see this woman set free from that which has held her captive?

Practice: Find and explore a "bent-over" posture. What does it feel like to hold that posture for any length of time? Imagine holding it for 18 years. Then, root your feet down into the ground and slowly rise to standing. Experience the freedom of being upright.

Take a deep breath...
               Exhale that which holds you captive...
                        Inhale freedom...
What holds you captive?
What does it feel like to be seen
        to be summoned
        to be spoken to
                with a power that frees you from captivity?
What does freedom feel like?
        Feel it in your feet
                Feel it in your back
                        Feel it in your neck and arms
Feel it throughout your entire body... *Freedom!*

Songs: *Freedom* by Klaus Kuehn
        Freedom Reigns by Rita Springer

Practice Journal
Body ➴ Mind ➶ Soul

"Which of the two did what his father wanted?"

Passage: Matthew 21:28-32

Context: This story is referred to as "The Parable of the Two Sons." Jesus is teaching in the temple courts when he tells the story of two sons: one who when asked to go work in the father's field said no, but later changed his mind and went and did as the father asked and another who initially said yes, but never went. Of course Jesus wants to know:

"Which of the two did what his father wanted?" VOICE

Or: *"Which one did the will of the father?"* ESV

The obvious answer the crowd gives him is the one who actually went, and Jesus agrees.

By this point in his teaching career, Jesus has attracted the attention of the religious leaders. Unfortunately, at this point in religious history, the religious leaders were more interested in positions, power and politics than doing the will of their Father (i.e., God). Jesus compares them to the second son.

And the first son, you ask? He tells them that son represents the tax collectors and prostitutes—the untouchables and outcasts, those that the religious system has rejected.

Note: As Jesus draws more and more attention and followers, the religious leaders are threatened. These leaders have a complex relationship with their Roman rulers. They receive "rewards" from the Romans for keeping the people in check. The best of them are trying to protect their ancient faith. The worst, of course, are drawn into corruption and power.

Ruminate: Consider the corruption of the systems of power in our world today. I'm fairly certain Jesus would've been equally as frustrated today as he was 2,000 years ago. Ultimately Jesus had no time for people who jockeyed for position or argued about who was "in" and who was "out." "Influencers" may not have been a term used in times past, but I'm fairly certain Jesus would not have cared for the concept very much. In his mind, everyone is welcomed to the table. You don't have to be a person of influence or clout to be a part of his community or tribe. Jesus was simply looking for people who would follow the way of peace, love, charity, grace, mercy and compassion, especially with those considered "least" and "untouchable" in this world.

Practice: Explore gestures, postures and movements of opposition—reaching arms in opposite directions, for example. What does it feel like to be pulled in two directions at once? Explore the tension.

Take a deep breath...
                    Exhale rejection...
                                    Inhale acceptance...
The world's economy has bankrupt our hearts
There are no checks to the balances
All is left to corruption of power,
        possessions, politics, place and position
Today, I will commit to reject this system
        that has left the world empty and void of grace
Today, I will commit to
        accept the unacceptable
                touch the untouchable
                        love the unlovable

Songs: *Atlas: Three* by Sleeping at Last
        Come to the Table by Sidewalk Prophets

Practice Journal

Body ❧ *Mind* ❧ *Soul*

"Woman, Where Are Your Accusers?"

Passage: John 8:1-11

Context: In order to trap Jesus, the religious leaders drag a woman who's been caught in the act of adultery to the Temple courts where he's teaching. The law dictated that she should be stoned, but they knew Jesus had a soft heart for the "sinner" (one who didn't follow the law). They thought they could trap him in a predicament of either offering grace or following the rules. But Jesus turned their accusations back at them, forcing them to examine their own hearts and cruel intentions. He simply says that the one without sin should be the one to throw the first stone. Of course, the wise among them were the first to draw away, and eventually, one by one they all left, leaving Jesus alone with the adulteress to ask her:

"Woman, where are your accusers?" KJV
"Dear woman, where is everyone? Did no one step forward to condemn you?" VOICE

Note: If this woman was "caught in the act," then the letter of the law at that time would have required the man with her to be there as well. As the old saying goes, "It takes two to tango." So, the fact that he wasn't there indicates she was merely a dispensable pawn in their game of entrapment.

Ruminate: In this world today there are many accusations thrown around about others... some true, some false and mostly those that are a mixture of both. How do I react when I hear an accusation against someone? Do I believe it immediately without question? Or do I realize there are two sides to every coin? How can I act with more grace, mercy and non-judgment towards others?

Imagine you are there in that scene. Picture yourself in the shoes of one of three people: 1) the woman accused; 2) the people with stones ready to condemn her to death; or 3) as Jesus offering grace, mercy and non-judgment. Take some time with that imagery in your mind, and then ask yourself, "How does this affect the way I might respond to accusations about others in the future?"

Practice: Explore a posture on bent knee(s) with arms extended in front of you, palms up, offering or receiving grace, mercy and non-judgment.

Take a deep breath...
          Exhale judgment...
                  Inhale mercy...
          Exhale shame...
                  Inhale grace...
Imagine that with
      one small act
            each day,
you could create a world
of compassion, grace and mercy...
That with every act of compassion, compassion itself would fill the hearts of every person around you...
That with every act of grace, grace itself would grow exponentially...
That with every act of mercy, mercy itself would spread like wildfire across this globe...
Now, go be compassion
          Go be grace
          Go be mercy

Songs: *Be Love* by Satsang & Tubby Love
       What Wondrous Love Is This? by Chelsea Moon
         & the Franz Brothers

Practice Journal

Body ~ *Mind* ~ *Soul*

"What shall we say the kingdom of heaven is like?"

Passage: Mark 4:30-34

Context: The crowds have gathered around Jesus to hear him teach, and because so many came, he got into a boat, pushed out into a lake, and taught from the water. Again, using parables, he tells many stories and then he asks this question:

"What shall we say the kingdom of God is like, or what parable shall we use to describe it?"

And then describes the tiny mustard seed, the smallest of all seeds, growing into the largest of all the garden plants—so large the birds of the garden rest in its shade. As we have seen in other questions Jesus has asked, his parables often included farming imagery as the ancient Near East culture was an agrarian civilization. People understood seeds, plants, harvest, gardening and farming. He used this imagery as metaphors because he knew it would be memorable and relatable.

Note: Jesus also used the mustard seed imagery in another parable he told (see Matthew 17 and Luke 17). That parable talked about having faith the size of a mustard seed—faith that would grow so strong that nothing would be impossible for those that believed.

Ruminate: From the smallest of all the garden seeds grows the largest of all the garden plants... and even more, it grows so large it provides shelter and shade to the animals there... and that is what the kingdom of heaven is like. Jesus teaches that from the seemingly insignificant comes a thing of great significance. He teaches that heaven starts with the tiniest of things.

We all bring gifts to this world. Jesus said, "The kingdom of God is within you" (Luke 17:21). What gift do you bring to the world? What abilities, passions, creativity, acts of beauty and kindness can you bring to bear in a world so in need of love, light, kindness and compassion? Do your gifts sometimes seem tiny and insignificant? Like the size of a mustard seed? What if we began to give freely of the unique gifts we bring to this world? What if we began to sow these tiny seeds in faith, trusting that as we scatter and share, the world will be a better place? Trusting that in our own small and unique way, we can bring a little bit of heaven to our place here on earth?

Practice: Begin in a posture that seems small, where your body doesn't seem to take up much space. Start to move in a way that slowly begins to take up more and more space until you fill your mat, your room or your studio.

Take a deep breath...
Exhale seeds of doubt...
Inhale seeds of faith...
I will gather every seed
not to myself
but in order to scatter
with abandon
I will give of myself
I will not hold back
If I can be a small part
of bringing heaven to earth
then I will freely fling
every gift germinating within me

Songs: *Heaven Is a Place on Earth* by The Mayries
As It Is In Heaven by Corey Voss

Practice Journal

Body ↝ Mind ↜ Soul

"Where have you buried him?"

Passage: John 11:1-44

Context: In this story, Jesus has been told that one of his closest friends, Lazarus, is sick. By the time he arrives, Lazarus has died and his sisters (Mary and Martha) both confront him with the same potentially "relationship-ending" statement: "If you would've been here, my brother wouldn't be dead." They don't mince words. They've gotten straight to the heart of their pain, and they hold nothing back in this conversation with someone that they clearly feel has let them down.

Jesus is not only moved to tears by their grief, he is moved to action. He asks,

"Where have you buried him?"

They lead him to the tomb, where Jesus directs them to roll the stone away. And with the command, "Lazarus, come forth!" out walks his dear friend, risen from the dead.

Note: In earlier stories, we learn that Lazarus' sisters are two very different women. Martha is into "doing" and Mary is into "being." They couldn't be more opposite. However, when they meet Jesus with their pain, they both confront him with the same statement.

Ruminate: Setting aside any notion of Jesus as a wish-granting genie-in-a-bottle, imagine him as the kind of friend who gets things done—a problem-solver who knows how to set things right. Now imagine he shows up just a little too late to help you with your own problem or pain. How would you confront him? Do you speak plainly or hold back? And, either way, why?

And if he asked you where you have buried this problem or pain in your life, where would you lead him? What would you show him? Imagine he is asking you now, in this moment. See him moved first to compassion and then to action. How does he raise the dead, lifeless places of pain back to life again?

Practice: First, what does it look like to stand up for justice in a situation, problem or place of pain in your life? Explore a posture of strength. Second, what does it look like to move with hope towards a situation in your life in need of resurrection and new life? Explore a movement of hope.

Take a deep breath...

Exhale pain...

Inhale hope...

Are you willing to let the past be the death of you?

Of your spirit?

Your soul?

Or... Are you ready to step into this present moment

and beyond

with hope?

Every breath, an invitation to let go

of the past, the pain, the struggle.

And to breathe in new hope

and strength for a better tomorrow.

It's hard to let go

I know, I've been there...

But it's only in the letting go

that your hands are open to receive.

Songs: *Shiloh* by Audrey Assad

Resurrection by Nicol Sponberg

Practice Journal

Body ∼ *Mind* ∼ *Soul*

"Are you here in this place hoping to be healed?"

Passage: John 5:1-9

Context: In this story Jesus brought his disciples to the Pool of Bethesda near the Sheep Gate in Jerusalem. In Aramaic this pool was called "The House of Loving-Kindness" and was said to have magical powers—when the waters were "stirred" by an angel of God, the first one in the pool was healed. Thus, it was surrounded by people who were disabled, blind, lame and paralyzed.

As they came to this place, Jesus approaches a man who has been at this pool for 38 years and asks him:

"Would you like to get well?" NLT
"Do you truly long to be healed? TPT
"Do you want to be made whole?" NIV

The man answers with many excuses but in the end, Jesus tells him (or commands him, rather): "Pick up your mat and walk," and the man does just that!

Note: This place would have been considered "unclean" to the Jewish people, and yet Jesus brings his followers (who were Jewish) there on the Sabbath. Jesus was not hindered by the rules of the religious leaders. Archeologists have uncovered a place they believe to be the Pool of Bethesda.

Ruminate: First, imagine Jesus here in this situation with no regard to religious rules. What is his posture, his facial expression, the gait of his walk? Now imagine him approaching you and asking you this question: "Do you want to be made whole?" How would you answer? What area of your life would you like to be made whole? What excuses might you give? How would you respond to his command to pick up your mat and walk even though you've been unable to walk for 38 years? Picture yourself rolling up your mat and walking away from your own areas of unhealth and unwholeness.

Practice: From a prone, supine, seated or crouched position, rise up with a sense of strength, health, power, resurrection. Perhaps experiment with disengagement and reengagement of your leg muscles as you do.

Take a deep breath...
         Exhale disease...
                  Inhale healing...

In this moment,
let the seed of healing be planted in your mind...
     your body...
          your soul...
               your spirit...
Picture the Light of Divine Healing
        shining on that seed...
The seed breaks open
Roots grow...
        down deep...
                and keep growing...
Health springs up...
New life...
      reaching for Light...
        opening up...
            spreading its leaves...
              ready to receive.

Songs: *Heal* by Tom Odell
      Healer by Kari Jobe

Practice Journal
Body   *Body*   *Mind*   *Soul*

"Do you understand what I have done for you?"

Passage: John 13:1-17

Context: We are nearing the end of Jesus' life here on earth. He has gathered for the Passover meal with his disciples and rises to perform the act of a servant. He takes off his outer robes, picks up the water basin and towel, and begins to wash the feet of each one. There is some protest, but he insists, telling them they have no place with him if he doesn't wash them. When he's done, he dresses, returning to the table with those he just served and asks,

"Do you understand what I have done for you?"
And he begins to teach them what it looks like to serve others. No "Teacher" or "Master" is greater than those whom he or she serves.

In this story, Jesus is setting an example of what it looks like to serve others. All are called to serve, and leaders are not beyond serving others themselves. Jesus ends by saying, "If you know these things, and if you put them into practice, you will find happiness." (VOICE)

Note: Jesus and his disciples lived in a very arid and dusty region of the world. Culturally, the host's servant washed feet when guests arrived to keep them from tracking in the dust. They had borrowed the room for their dinner, so there was no one there to serve them in this way.

Ruminate: Not sure about you, but I'm a "roll-your-sleeves-up-and-help" kind of person—whether I'm low in the ranks or the one in charge. And if I'm honest here, I'm fairly suspect of a leader who refuses to get down into the trenches with me. I have often found they have no idea what it takes to get the job done.

Have you ever served or worked for a leader who refused to help or work alongside you and your fellow laborers? How was that for you? Did you ever feel like they demanded more than was possible? Did they acknowledge your hard work?

Now turn the tables... have you ever been the one in charge? Did you work as hard as those who were helping you? Or did you enjoy the rewards without the cost of your own labor? If you are a teacher or leader, how can we serve those who are there to serve us?

Practice: Find a movement or posture of humility. Imagine serving others from this posture. Imagine others serving alongside you in this posture. How does it feel to work from a place of humility and gratitude for those who serve others?

Take a deep breath...
Exhale thoughtlessness...
Inhale humility...
Exhale entitlement...
Inhale gratitude...
Every day I encounter those who serve
not only in my workplace
but at the coffee shop and the check-out line
Am I grateful?
Am I kind?
Help me lead the way
with appreciation and consideration
an attitude of gratitude
I roll up my sleeves...
I serve.

Songs: *What Love Really Means* by JJ Heller
Let Them See You by JJ Weeks Band

Practice Journal

Body ∂ *Mind* ∽ *Soul*

"Could you not keep watch with me for one hour?"

Passage: Matthew 26:36-46

Context: Jesus knows the time for his death is soon coming, and he takes his disciples to the Garden of Gethsemane. He leaves all but Peter, James and John—who he confides in, telling them his heart is "overwhelmed and crushed with grief" (vs. 38). He asks them to keep watch with him as he goes a little farther ahead to pray. He prays with great anguish, and three times he returns to his friends and finds them all sleeping... those he has taught and served can't even stay awake with him when he needs their support most. He says to them,

"Could you not keep watch with me for one hour?"

His disappointment and discouragement are palpable. Following this time of prayer, his disciple Judas comes with Roman guards and Jesus is arrested to stand trial—a trail which leads to his crucifixion and death.

Note: Gethsemane can be translated "The Oil Press." It was located on the lower slope of the Mount of Olives near the brook of Kidron. The name Kidron comes from the Hebrew *qadar*, which means "to grow dark" or "to mourn."

Ruminate: Think of a time when you were in a dark or difficult place and those closest to you let you down? I would daresay this has happened to all of us. Moreover, it is often tough to express our needs to others, especially when we are struggling. It's hard enough to ask for help. And then, even harder to articulate what we even need in those tough moments.

Now consider a time when you were in a dark or difficult place and just the right word was or deed was offered. Perhaps the person didn't even know you were "down-and-out," and yet they said just the right thing at just the right time. How did that word or action help you in that moment?

Finally, how can we more aware of others who might be struggling? How can we offer a kind word or simple action that might help them in their difficulty?

Practice: Find s posture or gesture of withdrawal or grief. Then explore postures of reaching out and imagine your need being met in a way that brings peace and comfort. Compare how these different movements make you feel?

Take a deep breath...
Exhale difficulty...
Inhale tranquility...
I am in my own Gethsemane,
the oil being pressed from me is costly.
I sit at the Brook of Kidron,
this dark place of mourning.
I am alone in my grief
all others have let me down.
Then... I remember
a word of encouragement
an act of kindness
perfectly timed.
It brings hope...
I see light in the darkness...
My dawn is soon coming.

Songs: *Better Days (Stripped)* by Dermot Kennedy
Constancy & Stay With Me by Salt of the Sound

Practice Journal
Body ∾ Mind ∾ Soul

"My God, my God, why have you forsaken me?"

Passage: Mark 15:33-41

Context: Jesus hangs on a cross, nails driven through his hands and feet. Struggling to breathe, he gasps for every breath. Onlookers and passers-by would call out scornful insults, ridiculing those who were dying for their crimes. More heart-wrenching, his mother and one of his closest friends, John, stood at the foot of the cross, watching him die. Amidst this great pain Jesus cried out in Aramaic, *"Eloi, Eloi, lama sabachthani?"* which means,

"My God, my God, why have you forsaken me?" ESV

"My God, my God, why have you turned your back on me?" VOICE

Note: Even though the Roman ruler Pontius Pilate could find no fault in Jesus, he was pressured by the religious officials to put Jesus to death. Death by crucifixion was commonly used during Roman rule as a deterrent for crime. Crucifixion was held outside town where people coming and going could see the torturous form of death. It was a place of derision, mockery and contempt.

Ruminate: Are there times in your life when you've felt separated from or forsaken by those you love? ...from family? ...from friends? ...from God? What does it feel like to be rejected and alone in your greatest moments of pain?

Now imagine Jesus there, as your friend, in those places with you—as one who has faced great rejection and pain. Imagine him bringing you comfort, understanding and consolation as a friend who knows how to sympathize with you.

What does he look like? How is he dressed? Where is he seated or standing? What is the expression on his face? What does he do for you? What does he say to comfort you?

Practice: Lie on the ground with your arms extended to the right and left with palms up. This posture is commonly referred to as "cruciform"—it is a posture of vulnerability and surrender.

Take a deep breath...
            Exhale pain
                Inhale comfort
Though *you* struggled to breathe, Jesus,
        won't you bless me
            with breath
                that calms and soothes?
I breathe in your comfort and concern for me
I exhale all that brings me pain
I inhale peace like oxygen for my soul
I let go of shame, loneliness
            and the ache of my spirit
With every breath,
I receive healing for the broken places within
With every breath,
I unearth the resurrection of new life within
        With every breath...
            With every breath...
                With every breath...

Songs: *You're Gonna be OK* by Jenn Johnson
        O Sacred Head Now Wounded by Fernando
                                                Ortega

Practice Journal

Body ๖ Mind ๖ Soul

"Woman, why are you crying?"

Passage: John 20:1-18

Context: On the third day after the crucifixion of Jesus, the disciples and other followers have come to his tomb and find it empty. Confounded and confused, everyone leaves except Mary Magdalene, who stands at the entrance to the grave and weeps. Jesus appears, but she is blinded by grief and doesn't recognize him. He asks her:

"Woman, why are you crying? Who is it you are looking for?"

Thinking he is the gardener and that he has moved the body of Jesus, she asks where he has put him. And Jesus replies, "Mary," and as she hears her Lord say her name, her eyes are opened, and she finally sees him through her grief.

Note: It is important to note the significance of Jesus appearing first to a woman... in a culture where women were seen as second-class citizens. He did not appear first to one of his twelve main disciples who were men, but to a woman who has followed him and attended to his needs.

Ruminate: Mary has yet to understand... to understand the irony of thinking him a gardener or a grave robber perhaps. Her grief and sorrow has blinded her and keeps her from seeing the greater picture. And yet, it begs this question of us... How often does our own grief cloud our vision and keep us from seeing?

Now, consider your own seasons of grief, and then imagine someone you love calling your name. Not in a "time-for-dinner" kind of way but in a "so-glad-you-waited" and "I-love-you" and "I'm-so-glad-to-see-you" kind of way! Stop for a moment and hear this person call your name. As you wait outside your own empty tomb, in grief, sorrow and pain—hear them call your name.

Practice: Explore postures and movements of heartache and sorrow. Sense the weight and heaviness of lament. Then imagine someone you love calling your name. How does your body respond to being seen and recognized and pulled from your grief into joy and love?

Take a deep breath...
  Exhale your tears...
    Inhale the power of hearing your name...
How often
  has our own distress
    left us blind to the miracles all around us?
I'm afraid it is often.
For it is hard to see
  the resurrection power
    of Sunday morning
when all you know
  is the overwhelming fear
    of Friday's crucifixion
  and the blinding sorrow
    of Saturday's silence.
Who is it *you* have been looking for?
What did you expect to see, to happen?
  Why are you crying?
But listen...
  Do you hear the sound?
    Love is calling your name!

Songs: *Atlas: Sorrow* by Sleeping at Last
   Tears by Future of Forestry

Practice Journal

Body ⤝ *Mind* ⤝ *Soul*

"Who do people say that the Son of Man is? ...But who do you say I am?"

Passage: Matthew 16:13-20

Context: Traveling with his disciples he asks them who the people they have met as they traveled along have said that Jesus is. A variety of answers surface: John the Baptist, Elijah, Jeremiah or another prophet. Then Jesus asks those who've followed him closely,

"Who do you say I am?"

Simon answers, "You are the Messiah, the Son of the Living God." Jesus responds by blessing him and giving him the name Peter, which means "Rock."

Note: First note that "Messiah" means "Anointed One." Then note that this question is asked of his followers, not the general public. Jesus wants to know of his disciples— those who have journeyed with him—who they say he is based on their experience of and relationship with him.

Ruminate: People across the world throughout time and history have declared the person of Jesus to be many things—prophet, teacher, heretic, magician, divine, savior. Historians agree the man Jesus existed, but there is little agreement about whether or not he was who he said he was—the Messiah or the Son of God.

Take a moment to ponder your own relationship with Jesus. Who do *you* say he is? How has your answer changed as you've moved through this book and meditations? How is the Jesus the world has shown you different than the Jesus you've experienced on your mat, in your studio or your sacred space as you've moved and practiced with him?

Picture Jesus there with you asking you personally this question. How do you answer him? And what new name does he give you based on your response?

Practice: Enter a posture of contemplation and meditation. Take time to review and remember your experience with Jesus as you've moved your way through this book. How has he shown up for you differently than you expected?

Take a deep breath...
> Exhale pre-conceived notions...
> Inhale Jesus as he is...

Who do you say I am?
To one, I am teacher.
To another, I am prophet.
To yet another, I am friend.
To some, I am God.
To many, I am Savior.
But...
> *Who do you say I am?*
Who have *you* experienced me to be?
Not through the actions of another,
but through your experience of me,
> as I am,
> > as I reveal myself to you.

Please know that I love you...
I have always loved you...
And no matter who you say I am...
> I will always love you...
> > I will love you, even still.

Songs: *You Are Loved* by Stars Go Dim
> *House on a Hill* by Amanda Lindsey Cook

Practice Journal

Body ∽ *Mind* ∽ *Soul*

As We Move Out From Our Mats...

As we move *off* the "mat" (or out of our studio or meditation space) and move *into* the world, how can we move *differently?* How can we be changed by these questions of Jesus? Also, how can we treat others around us with more compassion, grace and understanding as a result of examining these questions?

We may not agree on who Jesus was and is, but can the questions he asked change the way we all interact with others every day? In the places we go? The things we say? To those we encounter as we journey?

It certainly did for his disciples.

And more and more, it is for me.

Before we part, I would be remiss if I did not share my own belief about Jesus with you. I am a devotee and follower of Jesus. He is my Savior and Lord. I have followed him since I was a young child.

When I was little, I experienced mysterious moments of divine wonder and curious discovery. On occasion those happened in church, but most often those happened outside... in creation... under the expanse of open sky or shelter of towering trees. It is in these moments that Jesus introduced himself to me. And these moments still happen today. When I take time to stop and pay attention. When I silence the chaos and commotion of this world. When I still my heart. And watch. And listen.

Over the years, as I grew in my religious experience, it became about helping and serving, which was good. But sometimes it was about following a set of rules and guidelines that left my mind narrow and leaning towards judgment. Oh, but God...

> *Perspective and life always shifts*
> *with the phrase that starts,*
> *"But God..."*
> *because God never leaves us in a place of non-growth.*

...But God wouldn't leave me in a space of judgment and fear, so he led me through what St. John of the Cross calls "the dark night of the soul"—a place of great anguish and spiritual desert-wandering. I have come out the other side of that desert a different person. And yet, on occasion, he sees fit to lead me back there again, for a refresher course of sorts.

For when I was little, I also experienced medical trauma at the hands of those who were there to help me. This experience has affected my way of being in this world, how I interact with others, and my view of this mysterious God. There are times when this wounding event attempts to overshadow all the places of mystery, wonder and curiosity. With Jesus by my side, I have worked diligently on the fragmented places of the deep, dark recesses left behind by that trauma. He has been a patient and tender guide on my healing journey.

So I can never truly say I have arrived.

Can any of us really?

And yet I can say I have returned from those dark nights, those desert wanderings, those deep fragmented recesses, to a place where I can stand again with a greater sense of wonder and curiosity. I have found the rules I once followed to be limiting and not accepting of others. I have found a deeper sense of God's presence in practices that other Christians have judged and condemned as wrong. I have also found profound healing in those same practices, and therefore, I know they are a gift of love from the Divine Source.

If you've experienced that same condemnation, judgment or trauma, I am sorry. I cannot speak for others' words or actions, but I believe in my heart that Jesus would be deeply saddened by the words and actions of those who have harmed us—those who claim to be his disciples as well as those who want nothing to do with him.

I pray in this book you've found a different Jesus than perhaps the one you may have encountered through *some* Christians and churches out there. That instead you've discovered a man who loved... and *loved* deeply... *accepted* the fallen and downtrodden with mercy... the saint and the sinner in equal regard... and *welcomed* those whom others would reject based on appearance, behavior or belief. That, in fact, you've found a man whose love drove him to a criminal's death on a cross to die not just for humankind in general, but also for you individually and uniquely... because he loves you.

The Bible tells us that Jesus came to the world to save the world, not to condemn it. That he came to save and redeem that which was lost. That he came to restore all that has been stolen from us. And all we have to do is say yes.

I stated earlier that Jesus is my *Savior* and *Lord.* Let me explain in simple terms what that means to me.

Savior means that I believe he saved me from myself, my places of wounding and trauma, and my own selfish desires and actions. In some traditions this higher level of being is attained through my own actions, accomplishments, achievement and abilities. With Jesus however, his heart of Pure Love flows through my own and a higher level of being in this world is dependant on him alone... and not me. Thank God because, frankly, I can be selfish and prone to rash judgment and negativity.

Lord means that I submit to his teachings and his heart of Pure Love towards me. I surrender my own desires to his and ask for his guidance in both the big and small moments in life. And as *Lord* he provides protection, shelter and a deep abiding peace in his presence.

If you should ever want that relationship with Jesus for yourself, all you have to do is simply say yes. Tell Jesus you desire to make him Savior and Lord in your life and that you want his heart of Pure Love to flow into and through yours. Call him Rabbi, and then let him teach you. Call him Friend, and let him love you. Call him God, and let his divine wonder captivate you.

I also encourage you to get to know Jesus better. One way to do that would be to study more about Jesus, starting in the Gospel of John, which can be found in any Bible app or at Biblegateway.com. I would suggest the following translations: The Voice, The Passion Translation, The Message or the New Living Translation (all available on Biblegateway.com).

Also, if possible, try to connect with others who practice Christ-centered movement and meditation. In time, perhaps you could also find a gathering of other Jesus-followers (a church, a Bible study or other small group gathering) to journey alongside you in this thing we call life on planet Earth. You might have to try several groups before you find the one that is right for you.

Ask Jesus to lead you, and trust that he will. And don't give up. Just because people love Jesus doesn't mean they have it all together or do a good job loving others as themselves. See, here's the thing: in order to love others as you love yourself, you have to learn to actually love yourself first... and we all know how many of us struggle to do that. We are, after all, only human. We must remember, in the words of my dear friend Anne, "We're all just learning here."

We started this book with a traditional Blessing of Loving-Kindness. I want to leave you with that same blessing...

May you be at peace.
May your heart remain open.
May you realize the beauty of your own true nature.
May you be healed.
May you be a source of healing for this world.

In Jesus name, Amen.

Godspeed on the journey, my friend.
Shanti Shalom, Jody

About the Author

For over 25 years, Jody Thomae has been involved in the dual paths of yoga and Christian ministry. While those two things seemed to be divergent paths, Jesus brought them together through her involvement with Healing Care Ministries and YogaFaith. She now sees them as two rails of the same track, leading in the same trUly BEaUtiful direction.

Her passion is for the revelation of Jesus to be made more real through creativity, embodied spirituality and healing ministry. It is her desire to portray the message of Christ's desperate and unfailing love for his people to help sustain the hearts of the broken and weary. She is particularly interested in the reclamation of the body in the healing of wounding events and works in the area of embodiment with survivors of abuse, wounding and trauma. She also leads a series of retreats each year focused on embodiment and spirituality.

She is the author of two books in the "Bible Studies to Nurture the Creative Spirit Within" series: *God's Creative Gift—Unleashing the Artist in You* and *The Creator's Healing Power—Restoring the Broken to Beautiful.* These interactive, in-depth devotional Bible studies are available through Amazon and Kindle. She also has a devotional CD, *Song of the Beloved,* available through most musical outlets.

Additional spiritual guidance, creative resources and inspiration can be found at jodythomae.com or on Facebook at facebook.com/JodyThomae. Learn more about her retreat offerings and embodied spiritual direction she offers at fullyembodied.com.

Reference: Spotify Playlists

For those who like worship music to accompany their practice, below are playlists for each question. First find and follow Jody's Spotify account **YogaFaith Jody.*** There you can find the playlists below that correspond to each question located under the "YogaFaith" folder.

Why were you searching for me?   YF Home
What do you want?   YF Overwhelmed
Why do you involve me?   YF Destiny
Who of you by worrying...?   YF Eye on the Sparrow
What good will it be...?   YF Cruciform & Bloodstained
What do you think?   YF Shepherd Psalm 23
What do you want me to do for you?   YF Letting the Light In
Why are you bothering this woman?   YF Alabaster Jar
Which is lawful on the Sabbath...?   YF Grace & Gratitude
Why are you so afraid?   YF Peace in the Storm
Who touched me?   YF Hem of His Garment
How many loaves do you have?   YF Be Still & Know
Will you give me a drink?   YF Living Waters
You of little faith, why did you doubt?   YF All My Hope
Why do you look at the speck of dust...?   YF In Your Midst
Do you bring in a lamp...?   YF Letting the Light In
Which of these three do you think...?   YF Flowing in Grace
If you love those who love you, what credit...?   YF Be Love
Now which of them will love him more?   YF trUe BEaUty
Should not this daughter... be set free...?   YF Freedom & Healing
Which of the two did what the father wanted?   YF Come & Listen
Woman, where are your accusers?   TSYF Defender
What shall we say the kingdom...is like?   YF As It Is In Heaven
Where have you buried him?   YF Rise up (Lazarus)
Are you here in this place hoping...?   TSYF Healer God
Do you understand what I have done for you?   YF Adonai Lord
Could you not keep watch with me...?   YF A Breath Away
My God, my God, why have you...?   YF Ps 22 Crucifixion
Woman, why are you crying?   TSYF Grief & Lament
Who do people say... Who do you say I am?   YF Jesus

*https://open.spotify.com/user/ppfbptvijasxp5zzsjd452upq?si=699194217b364e41

Reference: Practice Journal Prompts

Journaling Prompts for...

Body

What were the sensations of movement I felt in my body? (i.e., heavy, light, curled, open, big, small, powerful, weak, etc.)

Where did I feel these sensations in my body?

Did the sensations have a color associated with them?

If I could ask Jesus one thing about what I experienced in my body, it would be...

Also include movement or choreography notes.

Mind

What thoughts or questions arose as I considered or ruminated on the question Jesus asked?

What thoughts or questions arose as I considered or ruminated on the author's commentary about the question?

Where were my points of agreement/disagreement?

If I could ask Jesus one thing about what I thought, considered or ruminated on, it would be...

Soul

What feelings arose in me as I practiced?

Where were those feelings located in my body?

What were the sensations of the feelings? (i.e., heavy, light, curled, open, big, small, powerful, weak, etc.)

Was there a color associated with each feeling?

If I could ask Jesus one thing about what I experienced in my soul, it would be...

Made in the USA
Monee, IL
17 January 2022

89171086R00085